Table of Contents

Table of Figures

INTELLIGENCE SHARING, FUSION CENTERS, AND HOMELAND SECURITY

I. Introduction

Motivation

After leaving a civilian law enforcement career of seven years in 1994 to enter

Officer Training School as a Communications and Information Officer, I often wondered

if or even how the knowledge and experiences of these two careers could unite and play a

significant role in the National Security of United States. Then, September 11, 2001

occurred, a well planned, large scale terrorist attack within US borders. How could this

have happened? Did law enforcement fail to "connect the dots"? How did we not know

anything about this? As the facts started to come forth, it became clear that we, the

military, intelligence community, and law enforcement did miss several key indicators. In

the aftermath of 9/11, the reoccurring message that slowly began to emerge is that law

enforcement at all levels, including citizens and other civilian emergency personnel, must

work together with the Department of Homeland Security and the Department of Defense

to protect our homeland. In order that collaboration happen, leaders are asking for

improved intelligence, improved technologies, advanced networks, and clear-cut laws,

and appropriate funding--to make it all happen. Many issues became apparent during

research, three of which became the main motivators for writing this paper. First, in order

to truly protect the Homeland, America needs start looking at our "hometown"

resources—the eyes and ears of local police officers and citizens. Second, effective use of

cyberspace to "fuse" hometown information into usable intelligence is critical to our national security. Thirdly, leaders at all levels must understand this concept because ultimately, doesn't everything "rise or fall" on leadership?

Background and Purpose

The final report by the bipartisan National Commission on Terrorist Attacks (2004) concluded that the attacks on the September 11, 2001 were partly successful because information was not shared properly between agencies. Legal misunderstandings regarding foreign and domestic intelligence as well as the way information was shared between them contributed to the problem. Effective operations and counter operations were not launched because intelligence products were not collected into one, unified data document. Another reason is "federal intelligence analysts were unable to discern patterns of suspicious activity by the 19 hijackers because disparate points of data were contained in closely guarded databases maintained by individual intelligence and law enforcement agencies" (National Commission on Terrorist Attacks, 2004, pp 353,277). Indicators were apparently present, but they weren't seen because no single agency had the overall intelligence picture. As a result of the attacks, many efforts were initiated or planned with the goal of improving the sharing of information among the state, local, and federal authorities. For example, the USA PATRIOT Act, which became law in October of 2001, gave officials at all levels of government greater authority for gathering and sharing information. Additional improvement efforts included the creation of a National Criminal Intelligence Sharing Plan, which doubled the number of Joint Terrorism Task Forces and ensured at least one was located at each of the main FBI field offices. One key recommendation came from the Homeland Security Advisory Council (HSAC) Intelligence and Information Sharing Working Group, which recommended that "each state establish a multidiscipline information fusion center" (NGA Center for Best Practices, 2005). Other agencies introduced information sharing initiatives as well. For example, the Department of Justice (DOJ) and the Department Homeland Security (DHS) introduced secure computer networks and web-based services into the local, state, and federal agencies to help facilitate the flow and exchange of information. Some of the information systems implemented are listed below: (NGA Center for Best Practices, 2005)

- The Joint Regional Information Exchange System (JRIES) focuses on counterterrorism information shared by local and state law enforcement and the Department of Defense. It became operational in February 2003;

- The Homeland Security Information Network (HSIN) is designed to connect all 50 states, five U.S. territories and 50 major urban areas to the Homeland Security Operations Center and was introduced in February 2004. The HSIN incorporated JRIES and expanded its community of users beyond law enforcement and intelligence;

- The Regional Information Sharing System (RISS) program was originally established to combat drug trafficking and violent crime and now features six regional centers to share intelligence and coordinate efforts against criminal networks that operate across jurisdictional lines. It originated in the early 1970s.

These initiatives and programs attempt to fulfill the national objectives stated in our overall strategy documents. As mentioned earlier, securing the Homeland is arguably something that must begin at the local level. The establishment of fusion centers in each state is a critical part of that concept's potential to create actionable knowledge, i.e., meaningful intelligence, from the "raw" data collected from the various sources.

Most of this paper will deal with fusion centers and its challenges in supporting our National Security objectives. Occasionally, I will inject a few insights based from personal interviews and previous professional experience in domestic law enforcement. Although some of the civil liberties issues are briefly discussed, this paper is not meant to be an exhaustive discussion of those issues. Likewise, it isn't meant to list every agency involved in protecting the Homeland or its function within a fusion center. Finally, it is not meant to address all of the legal and privacy issues that have been raised regarding the collection of data within a fusion center. Even though emphasis is placed on the "bottom up" approach for achieving successful homeland security, it is understood that there still must be an effective "top-down" strategy with realistic, achievable objectives that guide other agency's strategies. We will briefly look at some of the governing documents as a foundation for further discussion.

II. LAYING THE FOUNDATION

Strategy and Plan Documents

The first main strategy document for securing the nation's homeland is *The National Security Strategy of the United States* (NSS). In order to defeat terrorist organizations that are organizing attacks against free societies, the NSS states that "we must make use of every tool in our arsenal—military power, better homeland defenses, law enforcement, intelligence, and vigorous efforts to cut off terrorist financing" (NSS, 2002). Law enforcement is mentioned five times in conjunction with strengthening intelligence warning capabilities as well analytical skills. It also states that "since the threats inspired by foreign governments and groups may be conducted inside the United States, we must also ensure the proper *fusion of information* between intelligence and law enforcement" (NSS, 2002, emphasis mine). In my opinion, that statement crystallizes the motive for fusion center development and provides the basis for continued emphasis for the trained intelligence analysts throughout all levels of government. The next selection discussed will be from *The National Strategy for Homeland Security* (NSHS).

The purpose of NSHS is to "guide, organize, and unify our Nation's homeland security efforts" to protect our citizens, critical infrastructures, key resources and leverage "all instruments of national power and influence." It stresses that to succeed, it will require national team effort that "leverages the unique strengths and capabilities of *all levels* of government, the private and non-profit sectors, communities, and individual citizens" (NSHS, emphasis mine). It goes on to mention the importance of cyber security as a "special consideration" citing the fact that most essential and emergency services, including critical infrastructures, need the use of the Internet to operate. Because of this fact, a cyber attack could be devastating to our mutually supporting critical infrastructures, our economy and national security. Securing the cyber infrastructure against all threats, natural and man-made, requires federal, state, local governments, and private sector to work together to keep cyber systems safe from exploitation and illegal use. Guidance for achieving those objectives is outlined in *The National Strategy to Secure Cyberspace* (NSSC), which will be examined next.

The NSSC establishes a framework for organizing and focusing efforts on the critical priorities, and it provides direction to all agencies that have responsibility in cyberspace security. Additionally, it identifies steps state and local governments, private companies and organizations, as well as individual Americans, can take to improve collective cyber security. This Strategy highlights the role of public and private engagement. It also provides guidance on how everyone can do their part to secure cyberspace. Due to the dynamics of cyberspace, this Strategy will certainly require adjustments and other changes over time. Moreover, due to the ambiguity and speed of cyber attacks, it will have to address the problems of distinguishing between the actions of terrorists, criminals, and/or nation states as well as finding the actual perpetrator. The main objective of the NSSC is to reduce our nation's vulnerability to devastating attacks against the critical information infrastructures and the physical assets that support them (NSSC, 2003). In order to meet this strategy's objectives, there should be an effective strategy to share information among all the agencies involved in securing the homeland, which leads to a brief overview of *The National Strategy for Information Sharing*.

The NSIS was released October 31, 2007 to "prioritize and unify our Nation's efforts to advance the sharing of terrorism-related information" (Press Secretary, 2007). It was developed based on input from members from government and private sectors from across the United States. It is intended to ensure that accurate, meaningful, and useful information is available to those who are charged with protecting our communities, both large and small alike. It is supposed to be able to accomplish those objectives by doing the following.

- Offer a structure for improved information distribution among the private sectors and state, federal, tribal, and local authorities. It should also help aid individual duties in securing the homeland.

- Describe how the federal government can support state and local fusion centers in major cities as well as help to fight crime in local neighborhoods.

More specifically, it touts the plan as actually enabling improved sharing of information across all levels of government and private sectors. It points out that before September 11, the government relied mostly on the competence of the Intelligence Community to process and transmit intelligence. Now, all levels of government, such as law enforcement, DoD, and DHS are active participants. The main method of sharing is via a concept called "fusion centers" that are owned and operated at the state and municipal levels. State connections to DHS and the military will be discussed later. Approximately 58 centers have been established or are in the planning phases. Additionally, improved information sharing with the private sector is a major concern partly because they own and operate over 85 percent of our critical infrastructure (Press

Secretary, 2007). Having laid the foundation for information sharing and strategies that

support it, fusion centers will be discussed in further detail in the next section.

III. INTELLIGENCE SHARING - FUSION CENTERS

Missed Opportunities:

As mentioned earlier, the 9/11 Commission Report noted that opportunities existed to possibly disrupt some or maybe all of the terrorist attacks that occurred on September 11, 2001. For example, Maryland State Police released a videotape of a traffic stop involving hijacker Ziad S Jarrah. He was stopped by Maryland State Police on a traffic violation, two days before he and 18 others hijacked four planes on September 11. Baltimore Mayor Martin O'Malley stated that local law enforcement officials should have been told that Jarrah was on a CIA watch list. Another example involves Hijacker Mohamed Atta, who was stopped and ticketed by Florida police in July 2001. He failed to pay the ticket and an arrest warrant was issued for him. However, when he was stopped for speeding again a few weeks later, he was released because the officer was not aware of the warrant (Candiotti, 2002).

Other missed opportunities regarding the failure to effectively share or analyze information were also included. Some of them are listed below (National Commission on Terrorist Attacks, 2004):

- January 2000, the CIA did not watchlist Khalid al Mihdhar or notify the FBI when it learned Mihdhar possessed a valid U.S. visa.

- March 2000: the CIA did not watchlist Nawaf al Hazmi or notify the FBI when it learned that he possessed a U.S. visa and had flown to Los Angeles on January 15, 2000.

- January 2001: the CIA did not inform the FBI that a source had identified Khallad, or Tawfiq bin Attash, a major figure in the October 2000 bombing of the *USS Cole*, as having attended the meeting in Kuala Lumpur with Khalid al Mihdhar.

- May 2001: a CIA official did not notify the FBI about Mihdhar's U.S. visa, Hazmi's U.S. travel, or Khallad's attendance at the Kuala Lumpur meeting

- June 2001: FBI and CIA officials did not ensure that all relevant information regarding the Kuala Lumpur meeting was shared with the *Cole* investigators at the June 11 meeting.

- August 2001: the FBI did not recognize the significance of the information regarding Mihdhar and Hazmi's possible arrival in the United States and thus did not take adequate action to share information, assign resources, and give sufficient priority to the search.

- August 2001: FBI headquarters did not recognize the significance of the information regarding Moussaoui's training and beliefs and thus did not take adequate action to share information, involve higher-level officials across agencies, obtain information regarding Moussaoui's ties to al Qaeda, and give sufficient priority to determining what Moussaoui might be planning.

- August 2001: the CIA did not focus on information that Khalid Sheikh Mohammed is a key al Qaeda lieutenant or connect information identifying KSM as the Mukhtar" mentioned in other reports to the analysts that could have linked "Mukhtar" with Ramzi Binalshibh and Moussaoui.

- August 2001: the CIA and FBI did not connect the presence of Mihdhar, Hazmi, and Moussaoui to the general threat reporting about imminent attacks.

These examples only offer a starting point for what might have happened if all agencies were made aware through proper information sharing. The only thing we can know for sure regarding this failure to "connect the dots" is that information was there in "a system" but it was not "fused" together into useable intelligence by all the agencies that could have "seen" the big picture unfolding to the point the appropriate authorities could have been alerted. As a result, the concept of creating "fusion centers" for every state began to emerge rapidly and take root in major strategy documents as a solution to the "connecting the dots" problem. Some of the common questions that usually arise when discussing this concept is: What exactly is a fusion center and is it really working as advertised? Are there problems or issues that hinder or put important information sharing capabilities at risk? Those questions and others will be explored throughout this paper.

What Is a Fusion Center?

According to *The Fusion Center Guidelines—Developing and Sharing Information in a New Era,* a fusion center is a successful and proficient instrument to exchange intelligence and information that maximizes resources, streamlines operations, and improves the ability to fight crime and terrorism by evaluating data from a diversity of sources. Additionally, they are a medium for implementing relevant parts of *The National Criminal Intelligence Sharing Plan* (NCISP). The NCISP is the outline for law enforcement managers to follow when putting together an intelligence gathering task force or capability. It has over 25 proposals that were examined by law enforcement officials and experts from all levels of governmental agencies. The main pillars of these guidelines are community policing, intelligence-led policing, and collaboration. Fusion centers can be further defined as "collaborative effort of two or more agencies that provide resources, expertise, and information to the center with the goal of maximizing their ability to detect, prevent, investigate, and respond to criminal and terrorist activity" (Fusion Center Guidelines, 2007).

Fusion Center Guidelines:

In order to help facilitate the development of effective fusion centers, the DOJ and the DHS collaborated in the development of 18 guidelines with the intent to provide a consistent, unified message to any agency wanting to establish a new center or modify an existing one. The following guidelines are discussed in detail in the source document but I will only summarize the ones underlined because they pertain to the thrust of my topic (Fusion Center Guidelines, 2007).

1. <u>The NCISP and the Intelligence and Fusion Processes</u>

2. Mission Statement and Goals

3. Governance

4. <u>Collaboration</u>

5. Memorandum of Understanding (MOU) Non-Disclosure Agreement (NDA)

6. <u>Database Resources</u>

7. <u>Interconnectivity</u>

8. Privacy and Civil Liberties

9. Security

10. Facility, Location, and Physical Infrastructure

11. Human Resources

12. Training of Center Personnel

13. Multidisciplinary Awareness and Education

14. Intelligence Services and Products

15. Policies and Procedures

16. Center Performance Measurement and Evaluation

17. Funding

18. Communications Plan

The first guideline, The NCISP and the Intelligence and Fusion Processes, basically says that each center should perform all steps of the intelligence and fusion processes and adhere to specific guidelines that are sector-specific. The NCISP is founded on the concept of intelligence-led policing (discussed later) and encourages law enforcement agencies to support and incorporate intelligence-led policing fundamentals in their efforts.

The second guideline is collaboration. Basically, it means creating a mutually shared environment among all levels of law enforcement, public safety agencies and the private sector for the exchange of intelligence and information. The objective is to leverage experience and resources while improving the capability to identify, thwart, and apprehend terrorists and other criminals. The development of a collaborative atmosphere builds trust and strengthens partnerships as well as providing individual ownership in the overall mission and objectives of the fusion center. The NCISP states that "Sharing is founded upon trust between the information provider and the intelligence consumer" (NCISP, 2004). Since trust is something cultivated on an interpersonal level, law enforcement task forces and other joint missions should be located within the same work area so they can work together on common objectives (NCISP, 2004).

Third, in order to really maximize the information sharing concept, the fusion centers must attempt to leverage any databases, systems, or networks made available by the participating agencies. I found this part of the fusion center concept to be the most controversial in regard to privacy issues, with the American Civil Liberties Union being one of the most vocal opponents. It is recommended that fusion centers gain access and connectivity to a wide variety of databases. The following types are examples and not meant to be all inclusive: Health and Public Health-Related Databases (Public Health

Information Network, Health Alert Network), driver's license, motor vehicle registration, location information (addresses and phone numbers), law enforcement databases, National Crime Information Center (NCIC), Terrorist Screening Center (TSC), criminal justice agencies, and private sources, such as security industry databases, identity theft databases, and gaming industry databases. Other database systems that support fusion centers and are available to law enforcement include the following: Regional Information Sharing Systems (RISS)/Law Enforcement Online (LEO), DHS' Homeland Security Information Network (HSIN), sex offender registries and corrections (Fusion Center Guidelines, 2007). With all that information potentially available to government officials, it really is no surprise that many people would have privacy concerns. As mentioned earlier, the ACLU has identified several concerns which will be discussed next.

ACLU Concerns

The first issue is fusion centers have indistinct lines of authority. Since so many agencies are participating in the fusion centers, it allows authorities to manipulate any disparities found the in laws that govern each level of government, from the tribal to the federal. ACLU's opinion, this is a blatant attempt to collect as much information as possible, while avoiding needed oversight and liability. In other words, authorities can pick and choose which laws to use that best suit them at the time. Second, with the participation of the private sector, the fusion centers are able to incorporate more sensitive information thereby increasing the risk of legal violations. Third, the ACLU believes that using the military within the fusion center along with the use of "data

14

mining" opens the door to repeat many of the privacy violations of the past. For example, the organization cites the history of abuse within intelligence units called "Red Squads", which became popular early 20th Century. Those units consisted of law enforcement and intelligence agencies as well as private corporations that joined together track anti-war, political and other social movements. Ultimately, a Senate panel investigating those incidents found the law enforcement personnel were in fact breaking the law. The excessive secrecy surrounding the current intelligence mission seems to limit public oversight and brings into question its real value (German and Stanley, 2007).

However, in hopes of alleviating privacy and civil liberty concerns with organizations like the ACLU and the American citizens in general, DOJ Chief Information Officer Vance E. Hitch addressed a senate subcommittee on those issues in April this year. He stated that the fusion centers operate under regulations that are designed to ensure that privacy information and the legal rights of citizens are protected:

> "As part of the Information Sharing Environment (ISE), Fusion Centers will be required to comply with the President's Privacy Guidelines for the Information Sharing Environment and other procedural, oversight and technological mechanisms established to protect the information privacy and legal rights of Americans in connection with the exchange of data with Federal agencies. Furthermore, an interagency effort to develop a unified process for the reporting, analysis, and sharing of information related to suspicious activities and circumstances specifically seeks to address how Personally Identifiable Information (PII) will be protected in these Fusion Centers and the ISE."
> (DOJ Hearing, 2007)

As a side note within the fusion center guidance, it does reiterate that fusion center members must ensure strict compliance with all local, state, and federal civil liberty statutes (Fusion Center Guidelines, 2006).

Finally, we come to the interconnectivity guideline. Its purpose is to help create a setting in which members seamlessly communicate by leveraging the development of future systems as well as those that are currently in existence. In order to allow for future connectivity to other local, state, tribal, and federal systems, it is recommended that everyone use the DOJ's Global Justice Extensible Markup Language (XML) Data Model (Global JXDM) and the National Information Exchange Model (NIEM) standards for future database and network development. The driving factor behind this guideline is interoperability—law enforcement authorities must be able to communicate. Eliminating barriers to communications and intelligence development and exchange is the ultimate goal. Incompatible computer systems as well as a lack of trust, interoperability, common terminology, driven at times by a lack of funding, are all forms of communication barriers. It is recommended that formal policies, procedures and standards be created to enhance communications. The leadership should communicate frequently and be responsive to the issues and concerns of all partners. This communication requirement becomes even more evident in DHS's Cyber Storm Exercise discussion in the next section.

IV. INTELLIGENCE SHARING AND CYBER SECURITY

National Cyber Security Division

The National Cyber Security Division of the DHS provides the federal government with centralized cyber security coordination and readiness functionality identified as needed in the NSHS, the NSSC as well as the Homeland Security Presidential Directive 7. It works together with public and private agencies to help secure America's cyberspace assets and critical infrastructures 24 hours a day, 7 days a week. One method to achieve this goal is to use risk management programs tailored specifically to cyber security. This process ensures that risks are analyzed, resources are prioritized and protective measures are implemented appropriately. Examples of current cyber risk management programs include promoting a National Awareness Month every October to all government and private agencies, implementing Software Assurance programs, deploying the Einstein network monitoring program, and conducting cyber exercises code named "Cyber Storm". Cyber Storm is a nationwide cyber security exercise that occurs every two years to evaluate preparedness in responding effectively to cyber incidents of national importance. Cyber Storm I and II, conducted February 2006 and March 2008 respectively, were DHS's first cyber exercises testing the ability to respond to cyber incidents across all sectors--private, international, state and federal. The following paragraphs discuss the Einstein Program and Cyber Storm exercises.

Einstein Program

The EINSTEIN Program is similar to an intrusion detection system (IDS) and was first implemented in 2004. It is installed outside an agency's network gateway and automatically monitors, records, and analyzes the flow of traffic in and out of the network, which allows DHS officials to identify anomalies that might represent hackers or other intruders (DHS, 2004). Einstein is supporting the White House Office of Management and Budget's Trusted Internet Connections (TIC) initiative, which requires all federal departments and agencies to reduce their number of gateways from approximately 4000 to a suggested goal of 50 by June 2008. Einstein will be deployed at the remaining 50 gateways adding an enhanced cyber situational awareness (Waterman, 2008). An example of Einstein's effectiveness occurred during a recent cyber attack on the Department of Transportation (DOT). The program detected unusual traffic patterns in DOT's network that were quickly identified, analyzed, and traced to the "attacker"— infected computer systems organized into a "botnet. Ironically, those infected systems actually belonged to another U.S. government agency, the United States Department of Agriculture (Miller, 2007).

Cyber Storm I

As stated earlier, Cyber Storm I was the government's first full-scale cyber security exercise of its kind. It included over 115 federal, state and local governments as well as four private sectors: information technology, communications, energy and transportation. The exercise allowed participants to respond to a variety of cyber and communications problems, and critical infrastructures attacks while cooperating with each other at the various operational and policy levels. It was designed to test communications, policies and procedures and to identify where improvements are needed in the event of cyber attacks. The following were exercised and/or identified:

- Interagency coordination through the activation of the National Cyber Response Coordination Group (NCRCG) and the Interagency Incident Management Group (IIMG)
- Inter-governmental and intra-governmental coordination and incident response
- Policies and issues that either hinder or support cyber security requirements
- Public and private information sharing mechanisms to address communications challenges
- The interdependence of cyber and physical infrastructures
- Awareness of the economic and national security impacts associated with a significant cyber incident
- Available tools and technologies for cyber incident response and recovery

The participants included federal, state and foreign governmental agencies as well as private sector partners from the IT, telecommunications, energy, and transportation industries. They each provided support staff to help plan and control the exercise as well as to ensure that their organizations' objectives were met.

The exercise simulated a complicated cyber attack campaign through several different scenarios aimed at various critical infrastructure sectors. The intent was to emphasize the interconnectedness of cyber systems with physical infrastructures and to test the coordination activities between the public and private sectors. The scenarios were developed with the assistance of industry experts and executed within a secure environment. The "enemy" objectives were as follows (DHS Training, 2008):

- To disrupt specifically targeted critical infrastructures through cyber attacks
- To hinder the governments' ability to respond to the cyber attacks
- To undermine public confidence in the governments' ability to provide and protect services

Cyber Storm I Results

The results of Cyber Storm I include the following eight major findings (DHS Press Release, 2008):

- Interagency Coordination: Interagency and cross-sector information sharing enhanced overall coordination, communication and response.
- Contingency Planning, Risk Assessment and Roles and Responsibilities: Clearly defined processes and procedures increased overall ability to plan for and assess situations.
- Correlation of Multiple Incidents between Public and Private Sectors: The cyber community was effective in addressing individual threats and attacks, but faced challenges in cross-sector situational awareness during a coordinated cyber attack campaign.
- Exercise Program: Ongoing exercises will strengthen awareness of cyber incident response, roles, policies, and procedures.
- Coordination between Entities of Cyber Incidents: Establishing expectations, roles, processes and communications in advance will dramatically improve coordination and response.
- Common Framework for Response to Information Access: Early and ongoing information sharing across governments and sectors created a common framework for response and strengthened relationships between domestic and international response partners.
- Strategic Communications and Public Relations: Public messaging is an important aspect of incident response and empowers individuals and industry to take appropriate action to protect themselves and the nation's critical infrastructure.
- Improvement of Process, Tools and Technology: Improved processes, tools and technology focused on the physical, economic and national security affects of a cyber incident will benefit the quality, speed and coordination of a response.

Cyber Storm II

Cyber Storm II, conducted in March 2008, was more comprehensive and dynamic than the first exercise. It simulated a large-scale coordinated cyber attack on critical infrastructure sectors including the chemical, information technology (IT), communications, and transportation (rail/pipe) sectors. The main goal of Cyber Storm II was to examine the processes, procedures, tools and organizational responses to a multi-sector coordinated attack via the global cyber infrastructure. The main objectives for this exercise were to test processes and concepts that were not covered in Cyber Storm I. The specific objectives of the exercise included:

- Examining the capabilities of participating organizations to prepare for, protect from, and respond to the potential effects of cyber attacks;
- Exercise strategic decision making and interagency coordination of incident response(s) in accordance with national level policy and procedures;
- Validate information sharing relationships and communications paths for the collection and dissemination of cyber incident situational awareness, response and recovery information; and
- Examine means and processes through which to share sensitive information across boundaries and sectors, without compromising proprietary or national security interests.

Since Cyber Storm II was intended to act as a medium for assessing communications, coordination and partnerships across critical infrastructure sectors, it allows participants around the world to participate from their respective office locations. The exercise control center remained at a DHS facility in the Washington, DC metropolitan area. The scenario progressed as players received "injects" through various means from the exercise control center. Those injects simulated adverse effects and allowed each agency to exercise their cyber crisis response systems, policies and procedures.

Participation in Cyber Storm II included 40 private sector companies, 18 federal cabinet-level agencies, 9 states, and 10 information sharing and analysis centers. In addition to the United States, the following 4 countries also participated: Australia, Canada, New Zealand, and the United Kingdom. The interaction between the public and private sectors in this exercise helped to accurately simulate the interdependencies of the world's cyber and communications networks (DHS Fact Sheet, 2008).

Cyber Storm II Results

Although the final results of Cyber Storm II are not to be made available to the public until August this year (2008), we can get an idea of some of the results from news interviews conducted with participating officials. Paul McKitrick, manager of New Zealand's Centre for Critical Infrastructure Protection stated in a news conference interview that he found the exercise more realistic than Cyber Storm I, since that one was primarily a "table top" exercise where as the latter had approximately 72 hours of real live exercise activity. His country had 30 organizations from the private sector and 10 governmental agencies with the main focus areas were on banking, energy, government and the information technology sectors. Overall, he found the exercise useful in testing his country's response plans as well as identifying areas for potential improvement (McMillan, 2008). Another insight came from participants at a recent RSA Security conference. Randy Vickers, associate deputy director of the U.S. Computer Emergency Readiness Team (US-CERT), said that there were still problems regarding information sharing. When there are problems with the Internet, communication is the still the critical element in formulating an effective response. Regarding the main purpose of this exercise, Greg Garcia, assistant secretary for cyber security and communications at the DHS, stated it was "fundamentally about identifying and responding to a fast-breaking cyber epidemic" (Jackson, 2008). Another item of interest was the importance of vendors during a crisis. Since they know the products best, it makes sense to build strong relationships with these vendors, especially those that support our critical infrastructures. Emphasizing that point was Paul Nicholas, a senior security specialist at Microsoft Corporation who said that making that cooperation work is not as easy as it sounds. He pointed out critical communications could be disrupted from something as "small" as not keeping a contact list updated. Vickers further stated that even though Cyber Storm II was more practical than the original one, it was not yet ready for other needed elements, such as a red-team enemy to make it more competitive. Again, specifics on the results are scarce sense the public report is not available yet and because participants had to sign a nondisclosure agreement to ensure potential vulnerabilities are not leaked to the public, but the overall theme was the "need for communication" (Jackson, 2008).

I think it is interesting to note that failure to communicate, at least in part, is a fundamental reason we missed opportunities to uncover the 9/11 plot. Also, communication problems were identified in Cyber Storm I and although touted as improved, it looks like it was still a fundamental problem in Cyber Storm II. At the molecular level, communication between cells is the basis for life. One could also argue that it is the basis for life in all organizations, from the family, to the private sectors, to the governments that run them. It should not be a surprise that after action reports of any kind will most likely mention communication problems. But isn't that fundamentally a leadership problem? Before exploring the main concepts of fusion centers, i.e., community policing, intelligence-led policing, and interagency relationships for information sharing, we need to take a look at the DoD, the primary agency responsible for the defending the homeland and how it fits into the fusion concept.

V. INTELLIGENCE SHARING - DOD

Department of Defense's Response

Much has been said about what went wrong with the failure of information gathering and the intelligence analysis processes that may have led to the failure to uncover the 9/11 plot, but let's look briefly at what the 9/11 Commission's Report says in regards to Department of Defense's response to 9/11 and the changes that occurred afterward. Specifically, as it relates to the connectivity to domestic intelligence agencies such as fusion centers.

According to the 9/11 Commission Report, the civilian and military defenders of the nation's airspace, FAA and NORAD, were not prepared for the attacks launched against them and could not put together an effective homeland defense against the attack. The report states that what happened that morning does not reflect dishonor to the NORAD's Northeast Air Defense Sector personnel. They did the best they could with the information they had received. The individual FAA controllers, facility managers, and command center managers made and flawlessly executed sound orders. They recommended a nationwide alert, stopped all local traffic, and ordered all enroute aircraft nationwide to land. On the other hand, senior military and FAA leaders had no effective communication with each other causing the chain of command not to function properly, which even included the President's ability to reach some senior officials. The morning events were over before the Secretary of Defense could enter the chain of command. Also, Air National Guard units, which had different rules of engagement, were

24

dispatched without the knowledge of the President, NORAD, or the National Military Command Center (National Commission on Terrorist Attacks, 2004).

US Northern Command

As a result of the confusion and lack of effective planning, U.S. Northern Command (USNORTHCOM) was established on October 1, 2002 to provide command and control of DoD homeland defense efforts as well as to coordinate with civil authorities. Establishing working definitions for homeland security, homeland defense, and civil support will help clarify and understand how the federal government protects the homeland. The following definitions can also be found in *The National Strategy for Homeland Security.*

Homeland defense is defined as "the protection of U.S. sovereignty, territory, domestic population, and critical defense infrastructure against external threats or aggression, or other threats as directed by the President." Homeland security is defined as "a concerted national effort to prevent terrorist attacks within the United States, reduce America's vulnerability to terrorism, and minimize the damage and recover from attacks that do occur." The statutory definition of homeland security also includes the "carry[ing] out of all functions of entities transferred to the Department [of Homeland Security], including by acting as a focal point [in handling] natural and man-made crises and emergency planning." Civil support is defined as "DOD support, including [the use of] federal military forces, the Department's career civilian and contractor personnel, and DOD agency and component assets, for domestic emergencies and for designated law enforcement and other activities"(Commission on the National Guard and Reserves,

Second Report to Congress, 2007). The lines between prevention and protection can often be confusing.

Civil Support Operations

USNORTHCOM is specifically charged with anticipating and conducting Homeland Defense and Civil Support operations to secure the United States and its interests. It's responsible for the air, land and sea approaches and includes the United States, Alaska, Canada and Mexico. Also included are the Straits of Florida and the Gulf of Mexico. Theater security cooperation with Canada and Mexico is also the responsibility of USNORTHCOM's commander. One of the benefits of its establishment is the consolidation of existing missions that were previously executed by other DoD organizations under one unified command. Even though it plans, organizes and executes homeland defense and civil support missions, it has relatively few assigned personnel. Additional forces are assigned as necessary to execute missions as ordered by the Secretary of Defense or the President. North American Aerospace Defense Command (NORAD), a bi-national command responsible for early warning and airspace control for Canada, Alaska and the continental United States, is also commanded by USNORTHCOM.

Some of the civil support missions include domestic relief operations during natural disasters, support with counter-drug operations and managing catastrophic terrorist attacks that might occur. One important note that affects the potential information sharing problem among domestic and military intelligence officials is that the Command can only assist the lead agency when ordered to do so because, in general, the Posse Comitatus Act of 1878 prohibits military forces to become directly involved in law enforcement. I will discuss that topic further in subsequent paragraphs. It is important

to note that in providing civil support, it generally operates through established Joint Task

Forces that are only activated when the emergency at hand exceeds the capabilities of the

local authorities and established lead agencies (USNORTHCOM, 2008).

USNORTHCOM Intelligence

USNORTHCOM's importance in the information and intelligence sharing with

DHS and all other supporting agencies in homeland security can not be understated, but

there are some legal boundaries that could effect the accurate and timely dissemination of

crucial information. LCDR Christopher C. Thornlow in his Master's Thesis, *Fusing*

Intelligence with Law Enforcement Information: An Analytic Imperative, points out that

each combatant command contains organizational directorates on its staff overseeing a

particular area. For example, "J3" focuses on current operations, planning "J5" focuses

on future planning and "J2" focuses on intelligence. USNORTHCOM J2, the

Intelligence Directorate, is primarily responsible to provide the Commander timely and

correct warning indications regarding threats pertinent to his area of responsibility

(AOR). With the correct intelligence, the Commander will be able prepare for a possible

attack and have forces ready to deploy in support of the civil authorities. The J2 mission

includes gathering intelligence from all sources available, including those from domestic

law enforcement agencies. He goes on to say that J2, with the responsibility for homeland

defense intelligence, has a twofold focus: analyzing intelligence threats outside the U.S.

and within its AOR. Because it is focused on both threats, it makes USNORTHCOM J2

logically suited to deal with the fusion of "traditional and non-traditional intelligence

information, creating that fused analytic picture for both the Commander of

27

USNORTHCOM and the rest of the Intelligence Community" (Thornlow, 2005). In March 2004, then Commander General Ralph E. Eberhart testified before the Senate Armed Services Committee regarding the USNORTHCOM's Combined Intelligence and Fusion Center. He stated the center "coordinates the acquisition, analysis and fusion of intelligence, counterintelligence and law enforcement information for the USNORTHCOM AOR and shares that information with organizations at the national, state and local levels" (Eberhart, 2004).

What are the legal issues regarding the sharing of domestic law enforcement intelligence with DoD officials? Thornlaw does a remarkable job in explaining the history behind the potential legal issues, but the bottom line is that the alleged legal problem does not really stop the flow of information gathered by law enforcement to USNORTHCOM's J2 counter terrorism analysts. Those analysts can view domestic intelligence on US citizens if there is a reasonable belief that they are engaged in "transnational terrorism" (Thornlow, 2005). At this point, it would be a good idea to discuss USNORTHCOM's formal link to each state, the National Guard.

National Guard

In response to 9/11, the Chief of the National Guard Bureau (NGB) coordinated the Guard's response nationwide. The NGB became a crucial link between state and federal emergency response capabilities and coordinated the deployment of 11,000 members of the Army and Air National Guard to assist law enforcement and other federal agencies in securing more than 440 of America's commercial airports. The National Guard identified volunteers to help defend critical infrastructures. Furthermore, it oversaw the establishment of weapons of mass destruction civil support team in each state while continuing to support the Army and Air Force's growing requirements for the deployment of National Guard units for the global war on terrorism.

Coordination Gaps

Clearly, the National Guard's role supporting the mission of USNORTHCOM is paramount, but in a recent study published April 2008 by the Government Accounting Office found that coordination gaps still remain between USNORTHCOM and the National Guard, both with the NGB as well as with each state. The study found that USNORTHCOM did have several ongoing efforts to improve coordination with the states and NGB in mission planning and responding to civil support requests. For example, during hurricane season it leads weekly conferences with the appropriate local, state, and federal emergency management representatives. It had also conducted two large exercises and participated in over 30 smaller regional, state, and local exercises each year to help responders prepare for natural and man made disasters. Additionally, they found that USNORTHCOM had involved NGB in planning reviews, but only informally. Although steps were taken to improve the coordination, gaps were identified in three main areas, as discussed below.

The first area gap was that USNORTHCOM officials didn't involve the individual states much in the development of its homeland defense and civil support plans. As a matter of fact, less that 25 percent of the state adjutants general reported that they were involved. Regarding civil support, USNORTHCOM officials stated that they are reaching out directly to states in order to understand plans and capabilities, but they relied on the NGB for state's perspectives for on homeland defense issues. Second, they found that USNORTHCOM was unfamiliar with state emergency response plans and did not have a procedure for acquiring this information. Fifty-four percent of the state adjutants general reported they thought USNORTHCOM was only slightly familiar with their emergency response plans. The fact that USNORTHCOM does not have a recognized and complete process for interacting with the states may contribute to this response. Since the information on the states plans and capabilities were not available in their planning processes, USNORTHCOM increases the risk that it will not be prepared to respond to an incident with all the needed resources to properly support the civil authorities. Third, an agreement dated in 2005 (which was supposed to provide the procedures for NORTHCOM and NGB to interact) does not clearly define the roles and responsibilities for each agency while planning for civil support and homeland defense. The lack of clearly defined roles and responsibilities has resulted in wasted effort, duplication of effort and overall confusion. For example, as required in NORTHCOM's homeland defense plan, NGB compiled the states' homeland defense plans and made them available to USNORTHCOM; however, USNORTHCOM planners stated they didn't request it or need access to that information. Without clearly defined roles and responsibilities, the study concluded that USNORTHCOM and NGB responses to an event could be fragmented and uncoordinated. Correcting these gaps should be a priority since it will help to integrate planning and coordination for catastrophic events as well as help USNORTHCOM's future mission planning efforts be more effective (GAO-08-252, 2008)

US Air Force Intelligence Support

In regard to cyber support, the Air Force is postured to lend its support in counterintelligence activities and information assurance. In January 2008, experts in the law enforcement, counterintelligence and information assurance met in St. Louis at the 7th Annual Cyber Crime Conference. The conference is sponsored by DoD's Defense Cyber Crime Center, or commonly known as DC3, and the Joint Task Force - Global Network Operations. Most participants attended for training and collaboration regarding how they can better coordinate efforts and respond to cyber-related threats and cyber-crime. There were several presenters from the Air Force; among them was Lt. Gen. Robert J. Elder Jr., the 8th Air Force commander responsible for Air Force cyber operations. He stated that being able to communicate, cooperate, and respond to threats is easier said than done. He also said one challenge is making systems easy to use but hard to penetrate by an adversary. Accurately identifying those who are attacking is another area for concern because it is can be extremely challenging. Finally he said that although there have been reports about linking China to attacks on U.S. systems, about 30 percent are linked to the addresses within the homeland. Because of the difficulty in locating the actual attackers due to IP address "spoofing", the Air Force is working on the technical and software issues needed to combat cyber threats and crimes. The AF is working to build its own force of military cyber specialists that are skilled in executing offensive and defensive operations. He placed a special emphasis on how the command relies on its partners in law enforcement, counterintelligence and information assurance to help identify and prosecute attackers (Petite, 2008).

To further clarify AF Cyber Command's relationship with local authorities, Lt Col S. Michael Convertino II, Director of Staff for AFCYBER (P), stated in an email interview that the AF is the Executive Agent of the DC3 and AFCYBER (P) participates in the National Cyber Investigative Joint Task Force (NCIJTF), through the Air Force Office of Special Investigations (AFOSI). (Convertino, personal communication May 30, 2008) The mission of DC3 is primarily to perform the following (DC3, 2008):

- Digital evidence processing and electronic media analysis for criminal law enforcement and Department of Defense counterintelligence investigations and activities.

- Investigations and forensic training to DoD members to ensure info systems are secure from unauthorized use.

- Remain on cutting edge of future investigations thru research, development, testing and evaluation (RDT&E).

According to Special Agent Paul Alvarez of the AFOSI, NCIJTF is its primary intelligence fusion center (Personal communication, June 2, 2008). It was created by the FBI with representatives from across the U.S. government to help stop criminal and terrorist activity. Shawn Henry, Deputy Assistant Director of the FBI's Cyber Division reinforced the fact that many criminals, terrorist organizations and other nations are looking to access or steal U.S. government corporate and military secrets. Additionally, foreign law enforcement agencies and the private sector are included to help support these goals. (FBI Weekly, 2008)

Posse Comitatus Act

The Posse Comitatus Act and the blurring lines between defense and security create other challenges. Those blurred lines could effect how fast and with what measure of force we respond to any attack on our nation. When applied to attacks on our critical infrastructures, it could be more confusing.

As discussed earlier, homeland security focuses on attacks within our borders while homeland defense focuses on exterior threats to our country. Can you imagine a threat that covers both? What if a cyber attack started outside our borders but the damage was done in the homeland? What about critical infrastructures? Which agency should respond? We know from Presidential Directive HSPD-7 and Strategy documents mentioned earlier, that critical infrastructures are essential for the nation's survival, therefore protecting it is a matter of national security (HSPD-7, 2002). Interconnected computer systems are the backbone of our nation's critical infrastructures. For the most part, the private sector relies on protection from private security firms and local authorities but they do not have adequate resources to protect their computer networks from serious threats, whether it is criminal, military or terrorist. Department of Defense networks tend to be better protected than civilian networks. However, since military networks rely heavily on the civilian internet for connectivity and information transfer, it creates a potential vulnerability. Arguably, since the nation depends on a secure cyberspace for protecting its critical infrastructure, i.e., its national security, the protection of these assets should fall on the DoD. However, criminal law normally presumes that a cyber attack is a criminal matter and not a national security matter. Basically, a cyber attack on a critical infrastructure network is presumed to be no different than an attack on a local business network .This presumption puts law enforcement in charge of the investigation which can often be slow due to the meticulous collection of evidence. That delay could prevent a successful response in confronting the cyber attack, even though it is an attack on our national security and could potentially cause catastrophic damages to life and property. Changing the presumption of attacks on critical infrastructure from criminal to a national security attack would raise several issues, one of which may require a new distinction between homeland defense and homeland security when it pertains to cyberspace. Another regards civil liberties which will be discussed later as issues regarding the use of intelligence within fusion centers (Condron, 2007).

Since we currently operate under the presumption that cyber attacks are criminal activities, law enforcement conducts the investigation in the same manner as with any other criminal act, respecting the civil rights of the suspected attacker, taking days or months to complete the investigation. For example, in February 1998, three teenagers hacked into 11 Navy and Air Force unclassified computer systems. Treated as a criminal matter, the law enforcement operation took nearly a month to identify and arrest the perpetrators, partly due to the fact one teen was located in Israel. If it was presumed to be a threat to national security, an aggressive federal defense action could have been started immediately and ended the attack. Even though nothing catastrophic occurred as a result, it highlights potential problems we could face responding to more serious types of attacks. In summary of the presumption issue, the bottom line is that if we are assuming attacks on critical infrastructures are a threat against the national security, federal authorities can act immediately to stop that attack. Once it is stopped, then the matter can be investigated in more depth to determine the true nature of the attack (Condron, 2007)

Changing the presumption regarding cyber attack threats from criminal to national security threats enables the DoD to be more directly involved in the protection of our critical infrastructures. Here again is where the Posse Comitatus Act of 1878 might apply. It is defined as follows (Title 18, U.S. Code, Section 1385):

> Whoever, except in cases and under circumstances expressly authorized by the Constitution or Act of Congress, willfully uses any part of the Army or the Air Force as a posse comitatus or otherwise to execute the laws shall be fined under this title or imprisoned not more than two years, or both.

The Posse Comitatus Act confines the federal military's role in performing traditional law enforcement functions without separate authorization. It was passed by congress due to the actions of troops in the South during the Reconstruction Era. At least two exceptions currently exist to the Act: emergency authority and protection of federal property and functions. The first authorizes quick and strong Federal action, including use of military forces to prevent loss of life or destruction of property. Also included in this exception is the necessity to restore government operations as well as public order when events disrupt the normal functions of local authorities. The second allows the use of military forces to protect Federal property and the functions of Federal government as required. At first look, the Posse Comitatus Act might appear to prevent the DoD from playing a major or lead role in protecting the homeland cyber systems of critical infrastructures (Conrad, 2007). All things considered, just about any response to an attack on most of the 17 Critical Infrastructure and Key Resources Sectors could be construed to meet the two Constitutional exceptions: Agriculture and Food, Banking and Finance,

Chemical, Commercial Facilities, Communications, Dams, Defense Industrial Base, Emergency Services, Energy, Government Facilities, Information Technology, National Monuments and Icons, Nuclear Reactors, Materials and Waste, Postal and Shipping, Public Health and Healthcare Transportation Systems, and water (DHS Prevention, 2008). Even if the two exceptions did not exist, one would argue that the Posse Comitatus Act would not hinder the military from engaging in the terrorist fight, including cyber attacks, in the homeland. The military has been involved in the war against drugs and illegal aliens so it is difficult to believe that we would have major issues with these types of laws. Congress can enact legislation or amend existing laws.

Now that the necessary link of collaboration has been established between key players needed for successful intelligence fusion, I will discuss the "eyes and ears" of intelligence collecting within the US borders—its citizens and local law enforcement.

VI. INTELIGENCE SHARING-LAW ENFORCEMENT

Intelligence-led policing

Intelligence-led policing is defined as follows:

"Intelligence-led policing is a business model and managerial philosophy where data analysis and crime intelligence are pivotal to an objective, decision-making framework that facilitates crime and problem reduction, disruption and prevention through both strategic management and effective enforcement strategies that target prolific and serious offenders." (Ratcliffe, 2008)

An interesting fact regarding this concept is that it has it beginnings in the United Kingdom. The police were starting to recognize that they were spending too much time responding to crime and not enough investigating the potential offenders. They started using more surveillance techniques along with gathering data from prospective informants. They found this method helped them be more effective in fighting crime. The news of this success quickly spread to other countries throughout Europe. After the terror attacks of 9/11, the process become well-liked in the United States and has been growing in popularity because of the emphasis placed on information sharing and "fusion centers" (Ratcliffe, 2008).

The intent of intelligence-led policing is to allow a more proactive instead of reactive approach to law enforcement or intelligence gathering efforts. It allows analysts or investigators to:

- Describe, understand, and map criminality and the criminal business process.

- Make informed choices and decisions.

- Engage the most appropriate tactics.

- Target resources.

- Disrupt prolific criminals.

- Articulate a case to the public and in court.

Intelligence-led policing helps increase public and private sector safety as well as providing insights into criminal activity trends. Additionally, increased information sharing with law enforcement contributes to crime prevention efforts within all the areas and agencies that are "plugged into the network". The end result of planning, information collection, processing, analysis, diffusion, and re-examination of information on suspected criminal activity is an information "product" called Criminal Intelligence. This chronological process is commonly referred to as the intelligence process or intelligence cycle. Although, there are various models of the intelligence process in use; most models will contain the basic steps that are outlined in Figure 1.

Collaboration

The fact that pertinent information was not shared properly prior to the 9/11 terrorist attacks has already been established. But is that when the problem suddenly became apparent? Some would probably answer "yes" to that question. However, the fact is that it did not suddenly become an issue as a result of 9/11. One of the most interesting facts discovered regarding the sharing of intelligence was located in a government report over 40 years ago. It recommended then that local and federal agencies should share information and collaborate better. That recommendation came from the Warren Commission's 1964 report on the assassination of President John F. Kennedy (Carter, 2004). Most of the commission's recommendations were directed to the Secret Service and FBI and it recommended they collaborate better with local law enforcement. Particularly, the commission called for increased information sharing and stronger liaison between local and federal agencies (Carter, 2004). Lessons learned from investigations over 40 years ago into that horrific event revealed our government agencies responsible for protecting us were not were functioning properly.

Hometown Security = Homeland Security

The International Association of Chiefs of Police (IACP) has a message they want everyone to know and fully understand: *"Hometown Security is Homeland Security"*. They are the world's oldest and largest nonprofit membership organization of police executives, with over 20,000 members in over 89 different countries. These leaders consist of the operating chief executives of international, federal, state and local agencies of all sizes (IACP, 2005). These executives became increasingly concerned that even with all the changes that occurred after 9/11, i.e., the PATRIOT Act, DHS, etc., it still left state, local, and tribal law enforcement ill prepared to meet the challenges of similar terrorist attacks in their respective communities. As a result, they created the *Taking Command Initiative*. This program brought law enforcement leaders from throughout the United States for a series of rigorous planning sessions to discuss what steps need to be implemented to actually improve homeland security from the "bottom up". It became apparent as the sessions went onward, that efforts at the Federal level have not led to "cohesive strategy that will allow state, tribal and local public safety officials to protect their communities successfully" (IACP, 2005). The main flaw in the development of their strategy was they did not seek the advice of the officials at the state, local, or tribal level. It became obvious to them that a new homeland security strategy should be developed that fully integrated the central roles of those agencies. Based on that, they derived five principles that must be incorporated into the national homeland security strategy to be effective in protecting the nation as a whole, from the local communities outward.

IAPC Five Homeland Strategy Principles

The five principles and a brief description are below (IACP, 2005):

1) *All Terrorism is Local.* Terrorist acts that occur within the United States are inherently local crimes that require the immediate response of state, local, or tribal authorities. Even large- scale and coordinated attacks that simultaneously impact multiple jurisdictions, such as the ones that occurred on September 11, 2001, require that state, tribal and local law enforcement agencies handle the initial response and recovery efforts.

2) *Prevention is Paramount.* For although the association agrees that there is a need to enhance response and recovery capabilities, such preparations must not be done at the expense of efforts to improve the ability of law enforcement and other security agencies to identify, investigate, and apprehend suspected terrorists before they can strike.

3) *Hometown Security is Homeland Security.* There are over more than 750,000 police officers who patrol the streets and highways everyday. Many of the successes in law enforcement are due the relationships built with the citizens of the communities they serve. As identified in the 9/11 Commission Report, terrorists often live and work in communities during attack planning and may have routine encounters with state and local law enforcement officials prior to the attack, as with September 11th hijackers Muhammad Atta, Ziad Samir Jarrah, and Hani Hanjour. Additionally, arrests of the Oklahoma City bombing suspects Timothy McVeigh and Eric Rudolph demonstrate how important local officers can be in the arrest of terrorist.

4) *Homeland Security Strategies Must Be Coordinated Nationally, Not Federally.* Many local officials were participating in planning and strategy development in the form of working groups, only which had little impact on the actually policy making decisions. As a result, the decisions that were downward directed were often seen as cumbersome and not conducive to their needs. In order to remedy that, all policy development efforts should be in the form of collaborative, equal partnerships and that of a working group type member.

41

5) *The Importance of Bottom-Up Engineering, Diversity of the State, Tribal, and Local Public Safety Community and Non-competitive Collaboration.* Basically, this principle stresses that an effective strategy needs to appreciate the diversity among the local communities and build a broad based security strategy that incorporates the means for others to be able to tailor it according to each of the their communities needs.

As I read through these principles, and the examples of failure to share information noted in the 9/11 Commission Report, I recalled my previous civilian law enforcement career and experiences with other state and federal agencies at that time. I can think of at least two main reasons we did not collaborate well then: usually it was due to egos and/or a lack of trust.

Interagency Relationships

The human factor in interagency problems between state, local, tribal agencies with the state and regional fusion centers as well as how those organizations relate with federal the agencies in working homeland security issues has been a topic of discussion for a very long time. While leaders of many of these agencies are trying to advance the collaboration initiatives, it appears that the "partner" and "team player" terms of endearment aren't actually as good as sometimes reported. It appears harder for the federal government to view the lower authorities as a partner in the truest sense of the word. They are more likely to be considered a subordinate and not as an equal. Another important observation to make is that relationship problems don't just exist between the different levels of government, but there also appears to be issues between law enforcement agencies, first responders and intelligence agencies. Leaders in the fusion centers often have to fight with the perceptions that the federal agencies do not understand their needs. The following is an excerpt from Washington, DC Police Chief Kathy Lanier's testimony before a Hearing of the Senate Select Committee on Intelligence, January 25, 2007. It reinforces the fact that cultural differences and misunderstandings exist between the federal, state, and local agencies, especially in regards to information sharing needs.

> "The Department of Homeland Security is not a law enforcement agency like the FBI … is a law enforcement agency … So it's very difficult for them to understand what my need to know is, if they don't know what it is that I do. If they're not familiar with what I do on a daily basis, what resources I have, and how I can reduce vulnerabilities through the daily activities of more than 4,500 employees here in Washington, D.C. … So a lot of information doesn't get to me, because they don't believe I have a need to know…I think it's just a lack of understanding. And this is not all DHS's fault … local law enforcement's just as much at fault. The Department of Homeland Security is not completely aware of what our operational capabilities are and how the information, if passed on to us, could be used to reduce the vulnerability … So information that may be shared with us is not shared with us because they don't think it's something that we can do anything with or that we can use to help reduce that vulnerability." (CRS, Options for Congress, 2008)

On a more positive side, Police Chief William J. Bratton of the Los Angeles Police Department delivered a speech at the 2008 National Fusion Center Conference regarding some of the successes he has seen interacting with federal and non-federal agencies in intelligence matters. He stated that participation by all levels of government is helping to increase the chance that patterns of both traditional crime and terrorism can be discovered. The speech also points out that for the first time in law enforcement history, fusion center environments have created an atmosphere in which federal government analysts are working together with state and local analysts throughout the other fusion centers. They are successfully working together to identify trends and share information with all the pertinent homeland security personnel in the public and private sectors. Together they are identifying trends and patterns and sharing the information with all homeland security stakeholders in both the public and private sectors. He said they are seeing "real progress" in removing the barriers and hindrances as well as in the development of joint intelligence products. The Chief believes that Washington is now realizing, more than ever before, that the approximately 750,000 sworn law enforcement officers among 17,500 different agencies at the state and local levels are better suited to deal with their local communities than the federal authorities. He said the main reason is because they really are the "eyes and ears" of their communities. The following excerpt of his speech reveals his satisfaction with the progress.

> "Recently, I had the pleasure of reading the first-ever intelligence product produced by the Department of Homeland Security (DHS), the Federal Bureau of Investigation (FBI), and the Joint Regional Intelligence Center (JRIC). I was impressed by the collaboration, the quality and the speed with which this product was produced. This was a tremendous example of the evolving partnership between the DHS, the intelligence community, and the Los Angeles Police Department. The result was …..[a] product that …… met the needs of the homeland security community throughout the country. Fusion centers are now partnering with Washington to address critical information needs tailored to their regions. This is but one success. There have been others." (Bratton, 2008)

Positive collaboration results are a good sign that the intentions of leadership are being implemented effectively. For example, in a key address to the first annual National Fusion Center Conference in March 6, 2007, DHS Secretary Chertoff described fusion centers as one of the main tools a community has to gather data that can potentially be used to protect its citizens and critical infrastructures. Even at that time, he made clear that the federal government had no intention of trying to control each center because they were a product of the state and local government that founded it. Additionally, he stated

the desired end result as follows:

> "Ultimately, what we want to do is not create a single [fusion center], but a
> network of [centers] all across the country, a network which is visible not only to
> us at the federal level, but as important, if not more important visible to each of
> you working in your own communities so you can leverage all the information
> gathered across the country to help you carry our your very important objectives."
> (CRS, Options for Congress, 2008)

However, one of the problems identified with keeping ownership at the state level regards

funding. The states may not have the money available to continue advanced intelligence

analysis and achieving the desired end state once federal funding expires (CRS, 2008).

The following paragraph outlines an example of how one state is experiencing that kind

of problem.

During an April 2008 phone interview with Chris Logon, Homeland Security and

Technology representative for the National Governors Association Center for Best

Practices, he identified several robust fusion state centers, one of which is the

Washington Joint Analytical Center. The WAJAC was create in 2003 with federal

funding and is responsible for serving as the state's central center for all terrorism-related

information, which includes the collecting and analyzing information as well as building

and maintaining partnerships will all private and governmental agencies to facilitate the

exchange of information. In January, a Washington State House Bill Report revealed a

$1 million shortfall due to the reduced federal funding. This shortfall has to be replaced

with state funds if it is going to keep the fusion center's 300 local agencies, 39 sheriff

departments, and numerous state and federal agencies together and effectively

functioning (HBR2506, 2008).

VII. CONCLUSION

Summary

The final report by the bipartisan National Commission on Terrorist Attacks (2004) concluded that the attacks on the September 11, 2001 were partly successful because information was not shared properly between agencies. However, information sharing did not suddenly become an issue as a result of 9/11. Lessons learned from the Warren Commission Report in 1964 indicated that local and federal agencies were not sharing information or collaborating effectively. It took another horrific event to recognize that agencies responsible for the nation's security were not communicating well. As a result of the 9/11 Report, intelligence fusion centers are emerging across the nation and are proving to be an effective intelligence collection, analysis, and dissemination tool for collaboration and information exchange among the private sector, tribal, local, state, and federal authorities as well as the DoD. U.S. Northern Command, the National Guard, and DHS are working to improve collaboration via national level exercises such as Cyber Storm I and II. Although the results of those exercises indicate communication problems still exist, there is progress.

There are many legal and privacy issues regarding the information sharing of domestic intelligence with DoD officials due to the Posse Comitatus Act 1878. However, most of them can be solved by Congress with amendments to or enactments of new laws. While legal and privacy concerns exist in balancing the need for National Security with the protection of Civil Liberties, the rise of fusion centers is an indicator that state and local law enforcement as well as public safety agencies have an important role to play in homeland defense and security. There are over more than 750,000 police officers who patrol the streets and highways everyday and many of the successes in law enforcement are due the relationships built with the citizens of the communities they serve. As identified in the 9/11 Commission Report, terrorists often live and work in communities during attack planning and may have routine encounters with state and local law enforcement officials prior to the attack, as with September 11th hijackers. Achieving true Homeland Security may be as simple as first achieving Hometown Security.

Further Research

While investigating this topic, other areas for potential research began to emerge. For example, vulnerabilities of the Homeland Security Information Network and network operations within an Intelligence Fusion Center are a cause for concern. If DoD and DHS are relying on "fused intelligence" to identify indicators of potential criminal and / or terrorist attacks, how easy would it be to disrupt operations at a fusion center? What critical infrastructures support fusion centers and are there back-up systems in place? Another focus area is the hiring and development of cyber analysts within fusion centers. How are they trained? How long does it take to attain competency? How are the positions funded? Are fusion centers adding critical infrastructure cyber analysts? Finally, the role of leadership in fusion center development and interagency relationships. What can be done to help overcome the lack of trust and build a true collaborative environment throughout all levels of government and the privates sectors supporting them?

BIBLIOGRAPHY

Candiotti, S (2002). Another hijacker was stopped for traffic violation. CNN, from http://edition.cnn.com/2002/US/01/09/inv.hijacker.traffic.stops

Carter, David (2004). Law Enforcement Intelligence: A Guide for State, Local, and Tribal Law Enforcement Agencies. available at http://www.cops.usdoj.gov/Default.asp?Item=1404

Commission on the National Guard and Reserves, Second Report to Congress, March 2007) available at: http://www.cngr.gov/pdf/CNGR%20Second%20Report%20to%20Congress%20.pdf.

Condron, S (2007).GETTING IT RIGHT: PROTECTING AMERICAN CRITICAL INFRASTRUCTURE IN CYBERSPACE. *Harvard Journal of Law & Technology*.

DHS, Critical Infrastructure and Key Resources. Retrieved June 5, 2008, from Department of Homeland Security: Prevention and Protection Web site: http://www.dhs.gov/xprevprot/programs/gc_1189168948944.shtm

Department of Justice, (2007).Statement of Vance E. Hitch. *Focus on Fusion Centers: A Progress Report*.

Department of Homeland Security, (2004). Einstein Program:Privacy Imapact Statement. from http://www.dhs.gov/xlibrary/assets/privacy/privacy_pia_eisntein.pdf

DoD Cyber Crime Center, (2008). Retrieved June 5, 2008, from DC3 Mission Web site: http://dc3.mil/dc3/mission.htm

Department of Homeland Security, (2008). Cyber Storm: Securing Cyber Space. Retrieved June 5, 2008, from Homeland Security Web site: https://www.dhs.gov/xprepresp/training/gc_1204738275985.shtm

Department of Homeland Security, (2008). Fact Sheet: Cyber Storm II: National Cyber Exercise. Retrieved June 5, 2008, from Homeland Security Web site: http://www.dhs.gov/xprepresp/training/gc_1204738760400.shtm

Fusion Center Guidelines: Developing and Sharing Information and Intelligence in a New Era, August 2006, 2, available from [http://it.ojp.gov/documents/fusion_center_guidelines_law_enforcement.pdf] (Source http://www.afcyber.af.mil/news/story.asp?id=123082700)

German, M, & Stanley, J (2007). *What's wrong with fusion centers?*. Washington, DC: ACLU.

International Association of Chiefs of Police. Criminal Intelligence Sharing: A National

Plan for Intelligence Led Policing URL:
http://www.theiacp.org/documents/pdfs/Publications/intelsharingreport%2Epdf

International Association of Chiefs of Police (IACP), Retrieved June 5, 2008, from About IACP Web site: http://www.theiacp.org/about/

Jackson, W (2008, April 10). Lessons learned in Cyber Storm II . Government Computer News, from http://www.infoworld.com/article/08/04/10/Lessons-learned-in-Cyber-Storm-II_1.html

McMillan, R (2008, April 10). Lessons learned in Cyber Storm II . InfoWorld, from http://www.infoworld.com/article/08/04/10/Lessons-learned-in-Cyber-Storm-II_1.html

Miller, J (2008). Einstein keeps an eye on agency networks. FCW, from http://www.fcw.com/print/13_16/news/102730-1.html

Waterman, S (2008). Analysis: Einstein and U.S. Cybersecurity. *UPI*, from http://www.upi.com/Emerging_Threats/2008/03/03/Analysis_Einstein_and_US_cybersecurity/UPI-23431204569280/

The National Security Strategy of the United States of America. (2002)
W House

National Strategy for Homeland Security
GW Bush - Washington, DC: The White House, July, 2002

National Commission on Terrorist Attacks. (2004). The 9/11 commission report: Final report of the National Commission on Terrorist Attacks upon the United States. New York: W.W. Norton

NGA Center for Best Practices, (2005). Establishing State Intelligence Fusion Centers. Issue Brief, from http://www.nga.org/Files/pdf/FusionCenterIB.pdf

Petitt, K (2008, January 17). AFCYBER brings its message to DoD's Cyber Crime conference. from http://www.afcyber.af.mil/news/story.asp?id=123082700

Press Secretary, (2007, October 31). Fact Sheet: National Strategy for Information Sharing . Retrieved June 4, 2008, from The White House Web site: http://www.whitehouse.gov/news/releases/2007/10/20071031-10.html

Press Secretary, (2003, December 17) Homeland Security Presidential Directive/HSPD-7. Retrieved June 4, 2008, from The White House Web site: http://www.whitehouse.gov/news/releases/2003/12/20031217-5.html

Ratcliffe, JH (2008) *'Intelligence-Led Policing'* available at http://jratcliffe.net.

Thornlow, C (2005). *Fusing Intelligence with Law Enforcement Information: An Analytic Imperative.*. Naval Post Gradutate School.

Title 18, U.S. Code, Section 1385 available at
www.law.cornell.edu/uscode/18/usc_sec_18_00001385----000-.html

USNORTHCOM, About U.S. NORTHCOM. Retrieved June 5, 2008, from U.S. NORTHCOM Web site: http://www.northcom.mil/About/index.html

U.S. White House, ''The National Strategy to Secure Cyberspace,'' February 2003; available at www. whitehouse.gov/pcipb/cyberspace_strategy.pdf.

VITA

Major Raymond R. Newbill III graduated from Covington High School in Covington, Tennessee. He entered undergraduate studies at the University of Tennessee in Martin, Tennessee where he graduated with a Bachelor of Science degree in Criminal Justice (with Honors) in June 1986. After severing as a civilian law enforcement officer for seven years, he was accepted to the Air Force Officer Training School at Maxwell AFB, Alabama. Following graduation in 1994, he was assigned to Defense Support Program at Lowry AFB, Colorado. Next, he was stationed at Scott AFB, IL with the AMC Computer Systems Squadron followed by a career broadening tour with the Recruiting Service at Hill AFB, Utah. His next assignment was as the Chief of Maintenance for the 4th Air Support Operations Group assigned to the United States Army V Corps in Germany. He deployed as the Air Force communication officer for the V Corps' close air support operations during Operation Iraqi Freedom in 2003, followed by one other combat tour in 2005. Prior to attending AFIT, he was the Technology Integration officer for the Air Command and Staff College at Maxwell AFB, Alabama.

APPENDIX

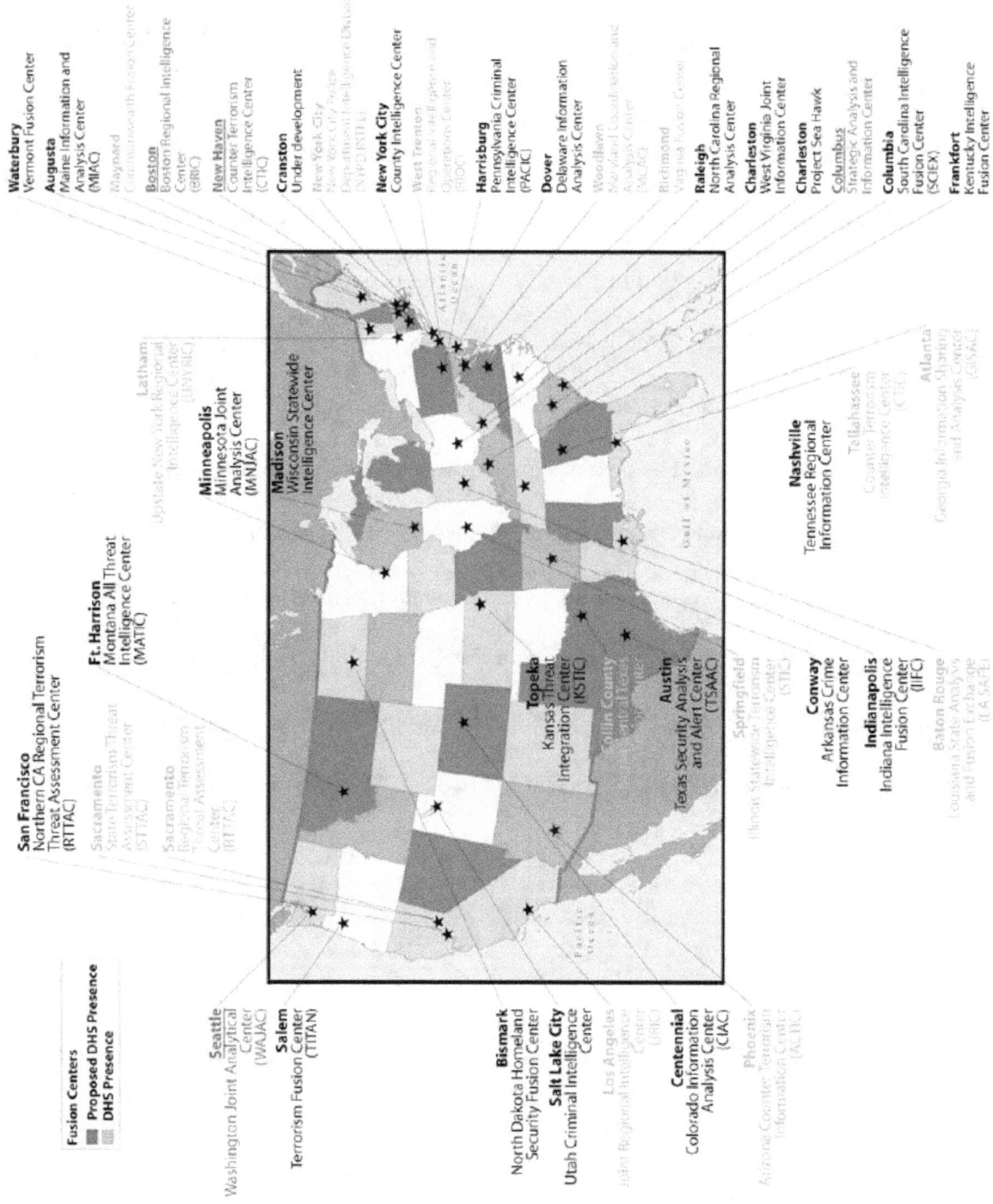

Figure 2 Fusion Center Map
(CRS, Options for Congress, 2008)

Figure 3 DHS Organization Chart
(CRS, Options for Congress, 2008)

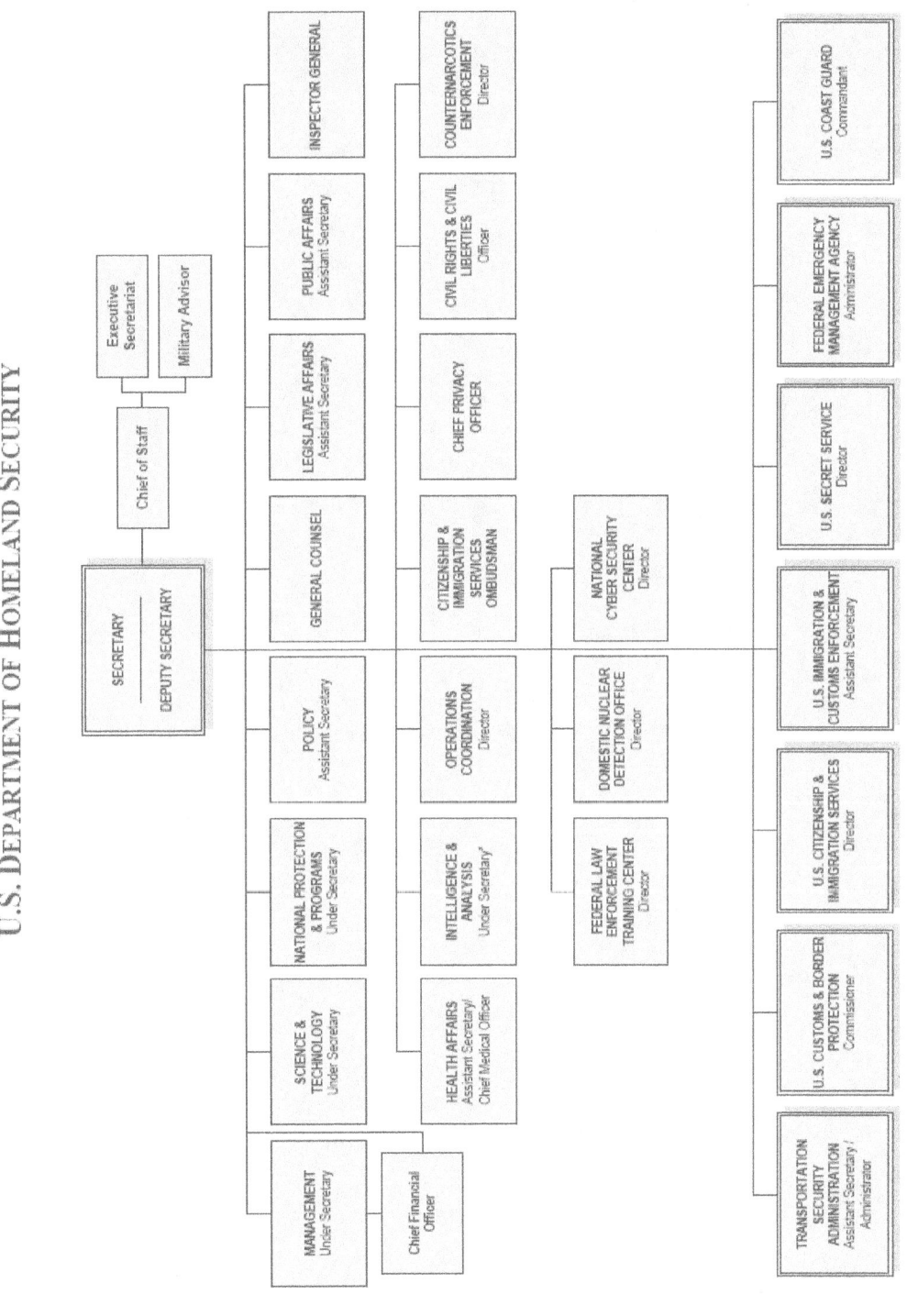

www.ingramcontent.com/pod-product-compliance
Lightning Source LLC
Chambersburg PA
CBHW080607290526
45790CB00007B/2667